SMITHEREENS

Also by Tariq Latif

Skimming the Soul (Arc, 1991)
The Minister's Garden (Arc, 1996)
The Punjabi Weddings (Arc, 2007)

Tariq Latif
SMITHEREENS

2015

Published by Arc Publications,
Nanholme Mill, Shaw Wood Road
Todmorden OL14 6DA, UK
www.arcpublications.co.uk

978 1910345 27 6 (pbk)
978 1910345 28 3 (ebook)

Cover image by Marcus Ward

Design by Tony Ward
Cover design by Tony Ward & Ben Styles
Printed in Great Britain by
4edge Limited, Hockley, Essex

ACKNOWLEDGEMENTS
Thanks are due to the following magazines in which
some of the poems first appeared: *Ambit, Assent, Bengal Lights,
Poetry Scotland, The Rialto* and *South Light* and also to Dunoon
Community Radio on the Luke Szymczak show.
The author would like to give special thanks to Tony Ward at
Arc Publications for his editorial guidance, and to the following
individuals for their comments on the early drafts of some of
these poems: Edmund Prestwich, Alan Johnson, Allan and Jo
Melzak, and Phil Lewis. Thanks are also due to Angela Jarman
for her contributions to the final draft and to Jennifer Woodward
and Phil Lewis for proofreading.
He would also like to give special thanks to doctors
Eva and Neil Thacker for their assistance during times of
financial hardship and to Alan Johnson for his kind gifts of
books which the author otherwise could not afford.

CONTENTS

For my very good friends
Alan and Ceri Johnson
for their kindness and support over the years,
with special thanks to Alan
for his "smithereens beneath our skins".

ARGYLL SYMPHONIA

I

Morning mist ascends
the giant cathedrals of the conifers.

Birds, in the low wintry light,
decipher the musical notes

left by last nights rain
and begin to sing new psalms.

*

A tired farmer faces the morning star.
A vixen in the woods licks her warm scar.
Bees in the meadows make liquid gold.
Seagulls fight over bread covered in mould.

The sun is sinking in an open scar.
The moon is melting in a milky mould.
The burn is bursting with petals of gold.
The snow owl gazes at the evening star.

*

Delicate fronds of mist
unfurl above the leaden loch.
Decaying plants, in the black
still depths, release bubbles that rise
and break the surface.

Thin threads of concentric circles
spread and fade like faceless clocks
or faltering pulses slowly foundering.

*

Patches of burnt golden grass
are crude crusts of light.

Patches of burning golden light
nourish crusty seeds of grass.

II

The hills shoulder
the shudders in the sky.
The air turns colder.
Thunder in the pouring rain
blunders on the slopes and boulders
like a giant, drunk
on spirits, falling over and over

*

The mist swirling
across the swaying sea of conifers
looks like torn sails of longships
lost in the raging forests of the sea.

*

The clouds, swallowing the sun,
fill up with the same colours
that seep from the autumnal leaves.

The trees, shedding the dry leaves,
fill with dreams that are light,
rootless, nimbus-full of flight.

*

Saffrons. Blood oranges. Rustic reds.
The leaves in the woods are burning
ever so slowly.
                    The trees give up

their ballroom gowns
                    leaf by leaf
to the caressing wind.

            The crumpled leaves
                    sweeping the air

look like quavers;
                    an allegretto of octaves.

The bare branches look like blank staves.

III

Two swans
gliding on Loch Striven
are like shadows of angels
or souls. The wide stretch of their wings,
near mirror images of themselves,
drip with dazzling
water.

*

The fox slumps
                        off the stump
        and creeps
                    into the coppery fern;
daubing the dead leaves
                        with berries of blood.

*

The blizzard scuffs up
spray across Loch Fyne.
Ballerinas in loose chiffons
vault into the vapourised air.

*

Dense mish-mash of mares tails
and bright sunlight sails
over the mauve mountains of Arran.

A rainbow surfs
across the cloud-cluttered sky

*

The only prints

in the snow

are mine,

the stag's and

his light-hoofed doe's.

IV

After days and days of hard frost
        and frozen snow,
rain breaks it all. How vivid
        and warm the colour of grass.
How delightfully musical
        the rain's whimsical laugh.

*

A grey New Year's Day.
Gannet high in the air
goes about its business
without any notion of a break.
Complete in the continuous life.

*

Trees are afloat
in a mist as dense as milk.

Grass is lost and the birds
are eerily quiet.

The regal stag surveys
the familiarity of the glen

with no sense of ownership
but of absolute belonging.

Taking his time,
he senses the subtle shift

between seasons by the warm
feelings in his spine. But the icy

wind in the vale has a sharp
glacial edge which he endures.

DIAMOND JUBILEE

Scents of sizzling onions and garlic topped
with chilli, haldi, ginger and salt, swirl
over the mowed gardens and neatly cropped
hedges. I'm listening to Sufi chanting
as I add a mix of three dals and twirl
them in the pot. A neighbour is putting
up a massive Union Jack. It unfurls
some fear in me since the far right spread hate

and lies while waving it with pride. And then
I'm ashamed of the Jehads who hi-jack
the phrase 'Allah-o-Akbur'. God is great.
I say it with each waking breath and when
I break bread. The flag and phrase say it all:
union in commonwealth or else we fall.

OSTEL BAY: SEEKERS AND FOOLS

Surfing the clear tides,
those thousands of crinkly curves
keep reconfiguring themselves
on the sliding surfaces of the sea.
Little pools, scattered around the cove,
are mini eco-systems disconnected

briefly from the whole; sea-anemones
rooted under rocks look like faceless
Medusas and those shells of sea-snails
are spirals of distant galaxies.
The oystercatchers wading
in the receding tides are pilgrims

foraging for manna; when they stab
at shells they seem to nod
at a vast watery wall. When the gulls
squabble over crumbs of crab,
they screech out
the names of Krishna and Christ.

True to their petty nature,
they miss the flurry of air sweeping
over the saffron brulée of the gorse
as a line of geese, with an impossible flight
mapped out in their collective mind, curves
in the sky like a fine necklace of pearls.

BY ECK

for Phil Lewis

Shallow rooted trees litter
the borders of Loch Eck. Thin
trunks, thick with moss, are easy
to cut and clear but seeds cast
by the wind will yield more plants.
My mind repeats unskillful
thoughts which could be weeded out.

*

Sections of Loch Eck sparkle
like pools full of diamonds.
Conifers against the light
look like Buddhists in quiet
contemplation. The deep glen
is full of emeralds and gold
that cannot be bought or sold.

*

On some windless misty days,
the still waters and hills deepen
and become Himalayan.
They have the same pure silence
that follows hours of brass bells
chiming, voices chanting and
eyes closing on attained peace.

*

A fawn with a golden sheen
crosses our path, looks
at us with steadfast stare and
for some shared seconds
our breathing becomes one
warm breath which spreads
through the wood, scatters as light.

My grandfather smells of sandalwood.
He has that soft glow of low light
and the blissful peace he used to have
after reading the Juma Namaz.*

His eyes, emptied of that fierce
determination to work himself out of poverty,
are full of blue skies after
days of hard rain, when wrestling
with his conscience he recognised
that material success, compared to the value
of a rich afterlife, was trivial.

I see him in my dreams
just as he was when I last saw him
in the streets of Lahore, a strong
dignified man with a presence
weighty as three sacks of wheat.

I know it is foolish to imagine him
bound in his body: after all,
a flute is just a piece of wood
without breath and fingers on keys;
a seed is just a sealed coffin
without soil, water and the warmth of light;
a body is just an assembly of fluids and flesh
without a soul, and a soul is more than just
the harvest of a life's wisdom –
it is to unite with the universal whole.

* Juma Namaz is Friday Prayer

FRACTIONS

Those ducks and drakes
                        dip their heads
           (like quills)
                              in an inky sea.
The tips of their bills
                    print
on the living air
                  musical notes
                         that are in key
between the acts
                of life and death.

Perhaps there is only light
or life, or both,
                (being the same) though this not proved
by Science as fact.

But here is a hint;
                the changeable emotions
between lovers and foes
                and how their story goes
cannot be predicted
                by any equation.

Here is another;
                the two swans
along the border
                between sweet water
and the Firth of Clyde
                are angels in disguise,
feasting on the free supper
                left by the receding tides.

That gull,
                spiralling through
the dull sky,
                slices the air
in thin loops and I sense
                        above my head the slight
pressure of other presences
                  living concurrently
      on the finer frequencies of light.

ONCE

for Dean Andrew Swift

there was a Christmas Eve
when street bands, playing steel drums,
ambled from street to street in an open
midnight mass and songs of praise were sung
around tables that were set with ample hot roasts
and the cross of Christ was a configuration
coded among the stars and there was this palpable
love, light as breath, everywhere
and we had sighed and smiled
and drunk without a single care.

.

MAY

for my father

Petals of the sun,
they burn,
brilliant yellow flames
in those abundant
bushes of gorse.

Scattered all round the glen
many coloured cups of nectar,
the promise of honey
undistilled, wild and raw.

Moss-scabbed stones,
black backbones,
break the water
into plumes of milk. Everywhere
the sound of streams cascading like chipped ice –
the sweet echoes of an Islamic paradise.

NASEEM

Her body, bound in white linen
and black belts, wriggles like a gigantic worm
as the men lower her into the coffin.

The women in black purdah
sing sections of the Quran.
And their soft singing, their meek singing
floats over the confinements of the coffin
and dissolves outside in the rush
and slush of commercial traffic
that does not stop or go slow,
not for the sleet or falling snow
or the passing of a soul.

Precisely at the appointed time
the men march in and take the coffin away,
abandoning the women whose singing
fractures into a dignified weeping –
except for the girl who moans and cries,
"may-ree ma, may-ree ma, may-ree ma…"

Around the amphitheatre of the pit
trees, smothered in snow,
look like the heads of women
with their hair flung and frozen
in a wild frenzy of mourning.
Or perhaps it is just the soul
whispering and wailing in the weak wind
as she watches her now-foreign cadaver
being buried in a foreign field,
and that notion of nationalism
being unpicked and smeared into ruins.

Silently and systematically,
the men shovel clumps of black earth
into the grave. The thump and scrunch
against the wooden lid becomes
a scuff and then a hush.

The Molbee, wiping soil
from his hands with some snow,
throws the white dust in the air.

Dry crystals shimmer
like hundreds of grated rainbows.

Note: *may-ree ma* means 'my mother'
Molbee is an Islamic priest.

Centre-stage in a den of blood hounds
he does not bristle, tense as a fox. He remains brave,
orders his pint, pays his hard earned pounds
and watches the dark body of the Guinness
settle like silt, like loose soil, like that fine
stuff he had shovelled into his father's grave.

He pays silent homage to his father
who had deliberately knocked on the doors
that had signs that read:
'No coloureds, no Irish, no dogs.'

And there are murmurs and whispered jibes
from the crowd of cowards all around him;
and they hated him before they had seen him
in their exclusive club, and they hate him
even more, now that he is deliberately
drinking his pint ever so slowly.

And after each mouthful
he lets the swirls in his glass
become still and he thinks of the stars
and of the Milky Way and of the greater cosmos
and how this tense moment will also pass.

No coloureds, no Irish, no dogs. He sighs
inwardly, knowing those signs have become
invisible, institutionalized. He looks long
at his empty glass and then makes sure
they see him raise his feet and shake
the worthless dust of that place
from the soles of his shoes,

and with his radiant soul intact
he leaves without once looking back.

Vadilal, preoccupied with financial concerns,
broods over the chopping board and shreds
the slices of coconut. Bhen turns
the half cooked roti over. Amrish threads
and clamps the tripod together.
His father adds oil to the mix of mustard seeds,
gram flour, garam masala and thin threads
of coconut. Amrish swivels the telescope and reads
the stars to locate Saturn. Scents of bread
reach us in the back garden where we sift
through space to pinpoint the faint
half-face of Saturn, haloed by a dark rift
and those bright rings. An unassuming saint
bound by gravity, as calculated by Newton's equations.
We cannot help but see ghosts of God everywhere
in that immense, immeasurable space, that utter
silence. Savoury scents release hunger sensations
and we are anchored back to Earth. From somewhere
Vadilal's voice calls us in for supper
and we set aside the past histories of the stars
to eat the spice-packed, steamed aubergines
that are as violet black as the sky at night,
that spill open like clusters of galaxies.
Rotis bend and fold like space...
and though Amrish has not seen
his father's living face
for a good few years now, sometimes in the stars'
dreamy light, he hears his haunting voice,
still calling him in for supper.

THE DESERT DAUGHTER

I bear my bruises like a second skin.
My face behind make up or a black purdah
would keep from the world my midnight moon.

If all of me were crushed into pure white tablets;
if I could fizz and dissolve as they do;
if I were to be drunk by God, processed and

ejected. Oh but I have managed a miracle
greater than walking on water; my head
and bones are helium-filled balloons.

I leave not a trace of a footprint
not a smudge in the sand, nothing
to suggest which way I have come,

or gone, or am. And because I find myself
among sand dunes, I wish not to hear the dry
voices of the desert fathers, not their empty

wisdom, not their apologies of abandonment.
I want the sweet singing of my sisters and
their many gifts of manna, zamzam and

the lightest light-filled sweetmeats. I want
to trade a rib for an angel; to be folded
snug among wings, held like a pearl, caressed

and kissed with a softness fine as drizzle.
I want angels with flaming swords to snuff
the blunt vaulting shadows that keep

cutting me. Oh that I should find myself
in this cubic igloo again. Again and again.
Is it night time? Why are my hands

and feet tied down like Christ's?
Do the men in white speak Latin or Aramaic?
They tease me with their shiny needles.

I should tell them how absurd
all of this is but they have transmuted
into mice. White mice with placid pink eyes.

SMITHEREENS BENEATH OUR SKINS

for Alan and Ceri Johnson

He was running over
the turfs of Moberley
while beneath his feet
lay the Lindow Man
waiting to be unearthed
with his undigested meal
and his boggy brown face
and his skull "split
in a deal done with the Druids
for a good harvest or two," and
as he draws a circle in the air
he concludes, "all sealed with a noose."

Chester Road which is some
five hundred yards from his home
was once a Roman road.

And he searches for shards of Roman pottery
from streams by small villages near Rome;
and he loves to touch
fragments from another time,
to sense in his blood the poetry
and pulse of another life lived long ago.

And I can still hear him
pronouncing the words
with precise weight and pause
from his selection of poetry and prose.

And the resonating words
dance in the air

like a swarm of bees

pollinating in our teenage minds
a passion for literature
a hunger for life
a discriminating taste
for the finer lights.

And he drags his daughters
over Dales and the hills of Wales
to connect with ancient sites and stones
never once dreaming that one of them

would halt the construction of Terminal Two
while men with shovels and pickaxes
all pause to watch the girl
scrape away soil from the artefact

releasing to the sky
atoms of ancient air

                    reaching to the girl
                    who had lost this vase

from as far back
as the Bronze Age.

                    Touching
                    the grain,

sensing the other girl's quick pulse,
that sudden loss
giving them goose pimples.

And here is the man
(out of time)
talking of the day
when as a teenager he ran
over the same piece of land

                              stampeding away
from the hedge

                              where his shears lay
          wedged

in the papery heart of a wasps nest.

Sunlight that is over eight minutes old
warms up the ancient stones.
His son is saying, " I do,"
to Miss Serrajotto who
is taking her vows in Latin.

And he describes in great detail
the man's feet in Caravaggio's
'Crucifixion of Saint Peter',
and how the anguish of injustice
affects him even now.

And he feels the nagging curse
behind the doubt in Hopkin's verse.

And somehow he connects
with some primeval fear
when, during the total
eclipse of the sun,
he finds himself
crying for no reason at all.

And it surprises me still,
even as he turns seventy two,
why he never picked up the pen
to detail his arguments
that have kept him agnostic.

HEST BANK

Sandpipers wading at low tide
bow and kiss the sea and sky.

Long loops of sky surfing the shallow tides
disappear near the sandpipers eyes.

Pools left behind by the receding tides
gleam like eyes full of fools gold and blue skies.

Sandpipers scouring the wet sand
keep a cautious eye on the Fujianese men

stooped to collect cockles for their gangmaster.
Lean as those birds, they work systematically,

sifting sand, shifting sideways, sifting sand...
Some of the men hum love songs

and pretend they are back home, harvesting
the paddy fields under a warmer sun.

Some of the boys cry quietly. The sandpipers,
finished with feasting, scatter freely.

The men drift in deeper
but the promised currency of their salvation

changes with the currents of the rising tide
and they are washed up on the shores of Hest Bank,

bloated with the sea and smeared with sand.
Sandpipers wading at low tide...

DUNOON BEACH

This darkness is table darkness;
the kind I used to love as a boy
when I hid, with my back
against the wall, under
the kitchen table. Nothing
could surprise me. I could see
all around by fractions, guessing
each person by their voice or clothes.
Even the sudden appearance of jinns
would not have unsettled me.

I know why our distant ancestors
lived in caves. Behind me there are houses
full of civilized caves. The stony beach
all along Alexandra Parade is under
the darkness of a gigantic table in the sky.
Somewhere above, great spirits of unflinching
faith feast on a banquet of light.

CHANA DAL WITH KEYYAH KADU

My dad's fingers are as glazed with water
when he does his wudu, as now, while he
drops chunky slices of Keyyah Kadu
over the sizzling onions, fresh ginger
and heaps of crushed garlic. He mixes in
coriander seeds, some salt, haldi and
lots of chilli. He drains the chana dal
adds it to the pan. Turning the heat to low

he goes next door for the Maghrib Namaz.
My mother and father, both Hajjis, turn
to Mecca and pray for my uncle who
has died. I stir the pot. Set the table.
We eat the curry with some masala.
I relish each mouthful and praise Allah.

Note:
wudu refers to the ablution performed by Muslims before prayers
Keyyah Kadu is a long green vegetable with a tough skin, akin to a squash
Maghrib Namaz is one of the five daily prayers and is the evening prayer;

GLORIA GILCHRIST

In memory of my partner's sister

She worked hard to make her mind become still.
Enduring the pain in her thighs and spine,
struggling with doubt and debt, she climbed the hill.

She turned to look down the forest of pine
and watched the breeze animate the bronze fern
into a rustling river of golden wine;

and she imagined salmon twist and turn
and hurl their bodies through currents of light
and she felt their bones in her bones burn

against gravity, with no notion of giving up the fight
in that original primeval pool of creative light.
And she sensed, in between the instantaneous flight

of jinns and angels, long before the breath
of dinosaurs and the waking of wilder beasts, the faintest
pulse of an expanding universe, the balance of death

against a play of life and light and that slightest
tipping of the scales in favour of the blood of Christ.

THE GROUSE

I'm an excellent judge of character,
he said, propping himself up on the stool.
I've only ever got it wrong once. Never
have I seen such stupidity. What a fool
to fall for a fantasy of Facebook chats.
Friend of a friend from uni. What pish.
It won't last. Mark my words. Facts are facts.
She's Scottish. Working class. He's an English
Paki lawyer from some place called Leeds.
They're chalk and cheese. I will relish
the day when she crawls home and begs and pleads
with you to take her back. I know you wish
she hadn't gone but she has to realize she is wrong.
Let's get an Indian. Vindaloo – I have mine strong!